100 THOUGHTS THAT LEAD TO HAPPINESS

ALSO BY LEN CHETKIN:
Guess Who's Jewish

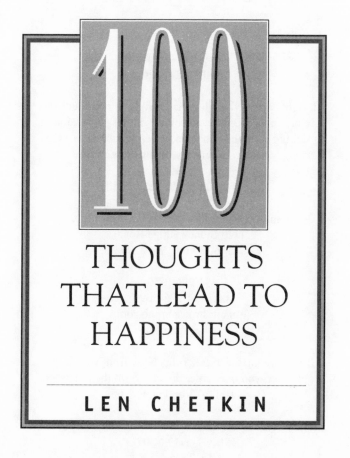

100

THOUGHTS
THAT LEAD TO
HAPPINESS

LEN CHETKIN

HAMPTON ROADS
PUBLISHING COMPANY, INC.

for the evolving human spirit

Cover design by Steve Amarillo

Hampton Roads Publishing Company, Inc.
1125 Stoney Ridge Road
Charlottesville, VA 22902

434-296-2772
fax: 434-296-5096
e-mail: hrpc@hrpub.com
www.hrpub.com

If you are unable to order this book from your local
bookseller, you may order directly from the publisher.
Call 1-800-766-8009, toll-free.

Library of Congress Catalog Card Number 2001097998
ISBN 1-57174-307-3
10 9 8 7 6 5 4 3 2 1
Printed in the United States

CONTENTS

INTRODUCTION

It's been twenty-five years since I first heard the words, "You back there, in the blue shirt, I have your father with me."

It was my first exposure to anything metaphysical, anything beyond the physical.

My soon-to-be wife had invited me to Lily Dale, New York, a spiritualist community located about fifty miles south of Buffalo, just off Route 60, that's inhabited by a great many mediums, one of whom was on the stage that day, in the auditorium, giving mini-messages.

"I have your father with me," the medium called out to me.

"I suppose that's possible," I answered.

"It's more than possible," she countered, "He's here, and he's showing me lots of shoes. Was he in the shoe business?"

My father had been in the shoe business most of his life.

And so the credibility began of knowing that not everything is as it appears on the surface. There's more. Much more.

And the "more" I speak of holds the answer to peace, security, and happiness in our lives.

As within, so without. Those four words compose one of the most powerful truths brought to mankind.

And I am almost ashamed to admit that it took me a lot of the twenty-five years since my first exposure to metaphysics to have that awareness crystallize in my consciousness. That what happens *within* is the determinant to what happens *without*. Carrying it one step further, in order to change our physical lives, we must look within for answers.

That's where meditation and prayer come into play.

Through meditation and prayer, we can change our thoughts. And with the changing of our thoughts comes the changing of our lives in the physical.

The Buddha says all we are is the result of our thoughts.

We are made by our thoughts.

If we choose to accept the Buddha's words as truth, then it would seem logical to monitor our thoughts.

After all, we have dominion over our thoughts, although sometimes we find ourselves saying "I can't help what I think."

We can help what we think. At this moment I choose to think I'm going to take a London vacation, that to root for the Chicago Cubs is to set yourself up for one hundred disappointments a year, that a pretty girl is like a melody, and that time and space exist as long as light exists.

So, if we have dominion over our thoughts, wouldn't it make sense to think thoughts that lead to happiness instead of thoughts that lead to sadness, depression, and despair? I categorically think so.

I was on a U.S. Airways flight out of Atlanta, bound for Buffalo, when the idea struck me! How many thoughts that lead to happiness could I list? I opened my flight bag, pulled out my pad and pencil and began to write.

Quite to my surprise, after filling out one page, I noticed two elderly women standing to my right watching what I was doing.

One of them asked, "What are you writing?"

"I'm writing thoughts that lead to happiness," I answered playfully.

"Oh yeah. What's a thought that leads to happiness?" she asked, picking up my playful attitude.

How about number one on the list?

1

SEND LOVE TO SOMEONE YOU FEEL HAS WRONGED YOU IN SOME WAY.

"Why should we do that?" she asked, with the playfulness subsiding and interest taking its place.

"Well, for one thing, carrying around anger robs you of peace and tranquility. After all, you started out peacefully, then you perceived someone did something to you that shouldn't have been done, and you chose to be angry about it.

"So another person has taken your power.

"Now you're walking around angry and resentful, and how long is that going to last?

"You chose to be angry, but there is the other choice.

"Love. And when love is introduced, the healing begins. For the other guy as well as yourself. And this way you remain tranquil."

The woman thought about it for a moment and then asked for a copy of the first page I had written.

She had been touched by the fact that she had a choice.

It isn't a given that anger must be returned with anger.

We don't have to act destructively just because the other person acts that way. We have a choice.

I know that this may appear to be a difficult concept to accept, but isn't it worth a try—what have you got to lose?

And as the women returned to their seats, after vowing to return for the copy they requested, I thought to myself, "Maybe I have something here. . . ."

I began to ponder number two on the list—

THERE ARE NO BAD GUYS.

When we take a good look at the "bad guys" who appear in our lives and analyze who they are and what they're thinking, we suddenly realize that they're teachers who have come along at precisely the right moment in our lives. That's what they are: teachers.

They present an obstacle to overcome that teaches us a lesson to be learned, forcing us to stretch ourselves because they stand in the way of the path that leads to our personal heaven.

They're an illusion that appears to be very real.

I remember standing in the doorway of my carpet store in Key West, looking out at the road being torn up. The city fathers had voted to "four-lane" Flagler Avenue, and anybody who had a business there had better beware. We were looking at six months of torn-up road.

I remember thinking, "Darn it. The business is just getting off the ground. Now what?"

I had a couple of choices.

One: I could visit City Hall and complain. Saying that to tear up Flagler Avenue would mean the finish of most of the small businesses located there. But I knew that wouldn't stop them.

Two: I could abandon the business and look for a new livelihood, because it would be impossible to survive once that road was completely torn up. Customers just wouldn't park three blocks away and overcome an obstacle course to get to my store. It was asking too much.

Three: I could look for a new location and hope for the best.

I chose number three. And it was to be a choice that would thrust me into a position of financial gain that no one could have foreseen.

So, where's the bad guy? It would seem the city fathers assumed that role.

But with everything played out, we discover that instead of bad guys, they were the instrument that forced me to move downtown (a desolate area at the time).

You could actually have called it a ghost town. As I think back, I say to myself, "It truly was a ghost town. *Spirit* was there."

And when the opportunity arose to purchase the largest building in downtown Key West, at bargain prices, just prior to the tourist business explosion, I now know that spirit was there.

Because I didn't have a dime to put down and still managed to acquire that building. So the city fathers, acting without concern for the business on Flagler Avenue, seeming to be the bad guy, in my case turned out to be the good guy.

Bad guys are actors in the play of life, and since we write our own script, where's the problem?

If we would just row our own boat and go gently down the stream, we would realize that obstacles appearing on the path are really teachers: forcing us to stretch ourselves as we reach higher.

Now, those are two thoughts that lead to happiness. And as I bring them to you, I am more convinced that merely by adjusting our thoughts, our choices in life, we can guarantee our own bliss, our own happiness.

3

USING OUR CREATIVITY RIDS US OF DEPRESSION.

When I was traveling around the country in a musical group, getting nowhere fast, I was often angry and depressed because of what seemed to be a no-win situation.

But when I finally stopped the music and created a carpet business out of a two-hundred-dollar investment, I used my time to enhance the carpet business instead of thinking about anger and depression.

I loved that business from the beginning, and when you love what you're doing, good things happen, because you are bathed in God's Light.

4

DON'T HURRY—DON'T WORRY—DON'T THINK TOO MUCH.

Egypt is a great place to visit. If you can get there, get there.

And please don't miss the Pyramid of Gisa. When you're at the Pyramid, visit the King's Chamber and the Queen's Chamber. Ancient energies are awaiting those who are aware.

I'll never forget the old man who had been hanging around the Pyramid for many, many years. His name is Champion, and he might still be there.

His words of wisdom were, "Don't hurry, don't worry, and don't think too much." Pretty good advice for a person seeking happiness.

5

THERE IS AN INNER VOICE SPEAKING TO YOU AT ALL TIMES. YOU'LL NEVER HEAR IT IF YOU DON'T QUIET YOUR MIND. LISTEN—MEDITATE.

The voice saved my life.

I was on Kennedy Drive in Key West waiting for the light to turn green so I could make a left on Route 1.

Just as it did, and I was about to go, a tiny voice in my head said, "Wait!"

"What do you mean," I thought. I hesitated and a car came speeding through the red light, going at least 60 mph. *Wow*, I thought.

After regaining my composure, I found that the light had turned red for me.

Then it turned green, and, again, I heard the voice, "Wait."

And impossible as it may seem, again a car came crashing through the red light.

Twice, within a period of ninety seconds, I was saved.

My mind is forever tuned in to the small voice that is talking to me.

6

FEELING DOWN IN THE DUMPS?
READ ABOUT LOVE.

The advice I'm speaking of has worked for me hundreds of times. I'm so happy it came to mind to include it in this book.

When you're feeling bad and dejected, pick up a book by

Alan Cohen
Deepak Chopra
Wayne Dyer
Marianne Williamson
Leo Buscaglia

And many others. They speak of love, and when you read about love, it is impossible not to have your spirit lifted.

7

NO MATTER WHAT YOUR SITUATION IN LIFE, YOU CAN CATAPULT YOURSELF INTO THE PLACE OF YOUR DREAMS.

The key is to believe—I mean believe—or to put it another way, to know of the world of infinite possibilities.

I know what happened to me. And now I know that another level is always there within reach. And another level after that.

Look at all the examples that you know of. The same possibilities are there for everyone.

Elvis Presley: from Tupelo, Mississippi to worldwide fame.

Colonel Sanders: refusing to accept failure, ends up with KFC.

Bill Gates: from his garage to billions of dollars in his possession.

There are endless examples.

Set your goal and take a step toward it. It can become a reality.

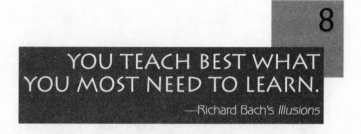

8

YOU TEACH BEST WHAT YOU MOST NEED TO LEARN.

—Richard Bach's *Illusions*

For the past thirty years, I have had this burning desire to absorb God's truths, and I know in my heart that if I were to lecture on them, they would be impressed in me as spiritual knowings, instead of just surface information.

Just repeating the words *Love, Forgive, Give, Go Within,* etc., and explaining their meaning, is a most satisfying thing in my life.

I can feel the peacefulness come over me as I write these words. Please don't miss this opportunity open to all.

9

LIVE NEVER TO BE ASHAMED OF
ANYTHING YOU'VE EVER DONE.
THEN YOU CAN GO ABOUT
YOUR LIFE WITHOUT FEARING
SOMETHING MIGHT SURFACE
THAT YOU AREN'T PROUD OF.

It's being impeccable, it's showing the people you encounter that you can be counted on to be an ally—never an enemy.

There's a good line: Always be an ally—never an enemy.

It's doing things that you know will enhance the quality of someone's life, and it's not doing things that carry a measure of destruction with them.

Everybody deserves a high quality of life. Everybody. Leave judgment out.

So, staying on a path of heal and reveal is going to bring the sweetness of life to you.

Then, you will be living without the fear of exposure. And any fear we can eliminate from our lives takes us one step closer to God.

WE ARE ALWAYS IN A HEALING MODE—PHYSICALLY, SPIRITUALLY, MENTALLY.

Even if you reject the idea of meditating (and I can't think of one good reason why you would), just closing your eyes and being still for a few moments will allow you to feel the healing going on.

Think about the healing you are absolutely sure of. Like cutting yourself with a kitchen knife. Do you have any doubt that the cut will heal itself? Of course not.

That is physical healing.

Mental and spiritual healing work in the same manner.

Have you recently gone through a divorce? Lost a loved one or suffered some other emotional stress? In most of these cases, time is the healer. Of course you never forget the lost loved one, but at least the emotionalism is reduced to a minimum.

11

HAPPINESS IS OUR BIRTHRIGHT.

Here comes love again. It seems no matter what we talk about on the spiritual path, love is the answer.

Because love is the most powerful emotion in the universe.

Love opens the door to happiness. Forgiveness is the key to love. Forgiveness of yourself and others.

When we forgive and accept the other people as they are, we are in the flow. To resist accepting them is to block the flow of energy. It's like rowing upstream against the flow.

Happiness will be yours. If you simply forgive.

WE HAVE DOMINION OVER OUR THOUGHTS.

We make the choices.
Read the statements of great men in history:

Lincoln: "I guess people are about as happy as they make up their minds to be."

Shakespeare: "There is nothing either good or bad, but thinking makes it so."

Thomas Paine: "We have the power to start our world anew (through thought)."

Buddha: "All we are is the result of our thoughts. We are made by our thoughts."

Jesus: "As we thinketh in our hearts, so we are."

13

SEEK THE SPIRITUAL, WHERE GOD RESIDES.

It is our personal life in the physical where sin, sickness, and death prevail.

There is no fear, no hesitation, no sickness, no stress, no negatives, when in God's presence.

In the Light we feel good. As a matter of fact, we feel exultant. And when we feel exultant, it is reflected in our physical life. Not maybe. But absolutely.

Find God and find heaven on Earth.

14

MAKE YOURSELF AWARE OF THE FABULOUS FOUR: GOD— TRUTH—LOVE—NATURE.

They are constants of existence and are with us moment to moment.

Close your eyes for a few seconds and enter the world of the spiritual—the world of the non-physical.

It's amazing how quickly one can enter the world of the spiritual. Simply by closing our eyes. Coincidence? I don't think so. God has given us a direct path to him/her.

First there is God, and then through God there is

Truth: the way things are

Love: unconditional, universal, non-judgmental

Nature: God manifested in the physical

15

FEELING SAD AND LONELY? SHOUT, "THIS IS GONNA BE MY DAY."

Because—just around the corner is the greatest day you have ever known. It doesn't matter how stuck you feel. No matter what your circumstances of life are. It's there, only around the corner.

The angels are always waiting for the opportunity to enhance your physical life. They are eager to be of help. They literally fight for the chance to be of help. That's how much they love you.

When you awaken in the morning, pay attention to everything going on. Gabriel will come to you in some form. Listen to your inner voice. The angels are speaking to you.

Everyone is yearning for that great day. Yours is coming.

16

TURN TO LOVE—AWAY FROM FEAR.

Love is what atoms are made of. The same atoms that make up a spaceship hurtling toward outer space are found in a tender daisy growing in your flower garden.

Since creation, all the atoms in the universe are love, pure love.

Not one is fear—not one! Fear has nothing to do with creation. It takes the Divine to create.

Fear dwells on the past. It rips at you, filling you with guilt that conjures up the past.

Love can lift you from the deepest despair. Send you soaring in the Light in a matter of a timeless, minute, micro-second.

Turn to love—love is God.

Fear is the ego, ever on the alert to latch on to suffering souls.

Not sure where to turn? Turn to love.

17

DON'T TAKE THINGS FOR GRANTED.

Ask yourself, "Am I taking all the things in my life for granted?"

I don't think there is a more important question you could ask yourself.

Taking everything for granted is robbing you of appreciation of wondrous events and the joy they bring to you.

Think of all the people, possessions, and events that happen daily in your life. Are they to be treated with disinterest, with a "So What" attitude?

What if, suddenly, it was all gone? Wouldn't you then awaken to the ingratitude you had shown God and wish all would be put back in place?

Of course you would.

Our lives are a series of miracles. Even the things we consider to be bad are actually learning tools for future use.

Take a few minutes to reflect over your life. Are you taking things for granted? If you are, you are making a serious mistake. What's happening is you are moving through life without the emotional highs and lows that contribute to joyous living.

18

LIGHT IS THE SHEEPDOG OF THE UNIVERSE.

This thought came to me after a morning meditation at a Deepak Chopra seminar. Since it came to me after a meditation, I gave it much credibility, because intuitive thoughts come straight from God.

During Mr. Chopra's lecture, the next day, I got a chance to raise my hand. He acknowledged me and I told him I had a thought that changed my view of the universe (the universe is a subject Mr. Chopra is profoundly interested in). He turned to the audience and said, "He said he had a thought that changed his view of the universe. I want to hear this." (tongue in cheek)

So I told him my thought: "Light is the sheepdog of the universe. What does a sheepdog do? He looks after the sheep. So when God said, 'Let there be light,' he was actually saying, 'Let there be an instrument to watch over and care for all that is about to come.' Now I feel that Light is with me in all of my endeavors."

Mr. Chopra said, "That is brilliant."

"I thought it was worth mentioning," I said.

The audience applauded. It was a great moment.

But the reason I mention it is to alert you to the fact that Light is also your companion.

I know you've heard, "Try to stay in the light" many times.

This is a confirmation.

THE MORE YOU GO WITHIN FOR YOUR ANSWERS, THE CLOSER YOU GET TO UNCOVERING THE AWARENESS OF YOUR DIVINITY.

Every time I sit quietly and reach a true meditative state, I sense myself being immersed in a limitless universe.

I love to ponder these key words . . . infinite . . . eternal . . . universal, because they bring God close to my heart. They aren't just words in a dictionary. They are the profound definition of every one of us.

Give it a try. Say to yourself, "I am divine, I exist in a spiritual world now. I don't have to wait until I pass on. I am immortal."

I have the ability to manifest what I desire in the physical world by use of my divine unlimited power.

I am spirit existing, for the time being, in a physical body.

20

IMAGINATION AND INSPIRATION STIR THE SOUL.

We can use imagination and inspiration as tools to experience the wonder of our goals and dreams as if they were already manifest in our lives. And think of the concerts and operas you attended, and wish to feel the emotional surge again. Through imagination it can be done.

When we turn up the light inside us (we all have one) through inspiration, our souls delight in the nourishment. Don't miss out on imagination and inspiration.

21

TAKE THE ROAD LESS TRAVELED.

The pathway of the singular is almost by definition the inventive pathway. Why follow the crowd and do what is laid out for you? So what if it's what everyone else is doing? How do *you* see it? That's the way to go. Robert Frost, in his poem "The Road Not Taken" writes:

> I shall be telling this with a sigh
> Somewhere ages and ages hence
> Two roads diverged in a wood, and I—
> I took the road less traveled by,
> And that has made all the difference.

As I look back over my life with a God-like view, seeing it all on an infinite straight line, in many ways I took the road less traveled and came out the better for it.

From writing songs
to selling shoes
to playing bass fiddle
to singing songs
to selling rugs
to lecturing on metaphysics
to writing books . . .

I don't know of anyone who has traveled this road. It's a road I've been happy with. It's a road less traveled.

IT'S EGO VERSUS SPIRIT: SUBDUE THE EGO—EXULT SPIRIT.

The ego believes in separation from God and others on the planet, and so competition is his thing.

It needs to be right.

It needs to be first.

It needs to possess things.

It needs the best of things.

It needs to win.

It hates losing.

It is never satisfied.

Give it everything it wants—it wants more.

It is insidious, always trying to impress on you to press ahead regardless of who gets hurt.

It feels it has to be better than anyone else.

Spirit needs none of the above.

Spirit is about peace, stillness, quiet.

Go within—feel the utter stillness.

Jesus said, "It is the father/mother within who doeth the work."

The ego can never enter the proximity of spirit. It drives it crazy. So go inside through meditation. And exult in spirit. Somehow, there's a spiritual cleansing in store for you.

WHAT YOU
RESIST PERSISTS.

Do you hate the way you look?

Do you despise the idea of having to work eight hours every day while your neighbor has started what you think is a cushy little business?

Do you bemoan the fact that you're driving a ten-year-old car while your friends drive new cars?

Do you hate your mother for any number of conditions she has instilled in you?

Do you feel you're unworthy?

Do you feel you're a failure?

Do you feel you're incompetent?

All of the above are aspects of resistance. The more you wallow in them, the greater they will become.

The key is to accept who you are. Stop resisting. Replace resisting with acceptance.

You are who you are and that's perfect.

Do you know how much energy it takes to resist all the things in your life that you consider to be negatives?

Accept who you are and go on from there.

Can't you feel the peace that comes over you when you suddenly realize there was no need for all this resistance.

Accept and take a giant step toward happiness.

THINK OF GOD AS TOTAL LOVE.

Instead of looking at God as a deity in charge of everything going on in the physical and having it stop there . . .

Instead of viewing God as a standoffish power who threatens to wield power at the slightest misstep . . .

Instead of thinking of God as a separate entity who resides somewhere outside of us, reigning over the universe with an iron fist and a loving heart . . .

Think of God as an integral part of our everyday living. The deity of which we are part and parcel. The mother/father spirit whose totality is the sum total of all souls everywhere, who can be called on at any given moment to aid any individual cause, and whose love is infinite and is never withheld, no matter what the circumstances, because it is our birthright, being divine, to call upon the infinite gatherings of love and once feeling love's existence, be immersed in it.

It's like not seeing the forest for the trees.

We are the trees.
We are the forest.
We are Divine. We are God.

DO WHAT YOU SAY YOU'RE GOING TO DO.

Want to hit the top?

Do what you say you're going to do.

Don't care if you slip to the bottom?

Don't follow through.

When you follow through on your promises, you are putting yourself directly in the flow of universal positive energy. You are rowing your boat gently down the stream. Without worry. Without anxiety. Without tenseness. Without distress.

There is no monkey on your back when you honor your commitment. God is walking beside you.

But don't follow through?

Don't honor your commitment?

Don't do as you say?

Then, you are listening to the whispering ego saying, "It's not necessary to always be true to your commitment. Take the easy route. Slide around it."

This is a sure way to committing spiritual, financial, and personal suicide.

Your life will echo the choices you make.

BE AWARE OF THE MIRROR OF LIFE.

When we open our eyes each morning, we are seeing a mirror of our inner dialogue.

The things we admire in someone are mirrors of qualities that exist in us.

It's fun to make it a task each day to watch for things we admire in people. If you have a problem finding things you admire, my bet is you need to change to more loving, positive habits.

Here's a scenario that recently happened to me.

I was wandering through a bookstore and came upon a book about Rosa Parks. I had always been interested in knowing what sort of woman she was. I knew she was courageous, because she refused to give up her seat in the front of the bus in the face of all that hostility. What was her background? Was she educated? Yes. Was she a woman of power? Yes. Needless to say, I bought the book.

One week later, I attended a seminar given by Deepak Chopra.

Mr. Chopra is highly respected in the field of metaphysics, as well as the field of medicine.

During the seminar, to illustrate a point (I've forgotten the point), he mentioned two of the people he most respected in life—one of them was Rosa Parks.

I was stunned. Only a week before I had purchased her life story.

It wasn't a coincidence.

It was the mirror at work.

27

COUNT YOUR BLESSINGS.

There is a spiritualist church in Lily Dale, New York called the Church of the Living Spirit. It was founded by my wife, Emmy, and a few of her friends. When you step inside the door, you can feel the love. You can see the people looking in each other's eyes and mirroring God's love to each other.

There are many wonderful songs being sung every Sunday.

My favorite is *Count Your Blessings*.

When you count your blessings instead of dwelling on misfortunes, you invite other blessings offered by God. There is no limit to abundance coming our way when we show our appreciation.

"Be grateful for what you have" is my wife's favorite advice to me. Stop focusing on what could go wrong. Instead, focus on what will go right.

With love in your heart, count your blessings.

28

SILENCE IS GOLDEN.

We've all heard the phrase.

Silence is golden. When a salesman does the pitch and knows when to stop and wait for the customer's response, the silence is powerful.

Silence is golden in the theatre when the actor senses when to pause and when to continue.

And silence is golden in meditation, when we quiet our minds to allow us to go beneath the surface of the everyday hum of scattered thinking and reach the subconscious and superconscious that bring forth ideas never dreamed of.

Ideas, that emerge in an orderly fashion, can be used to manifest your desires.

Oh yes. Silence is certainly golden.

NEVER JUDGE A MAN UNTIL YOU'VE WALKED IN HIS SHOES.

We've all heard this before.

Suppose you have a friend who seems to love playing practical jokes. And you hate it! But you never gave a thought as to why he does it. Maybe there are things tearing at him, things he feels he has no control over. So, he plays practical jokes to get even with society. He wants to make others look silly, because he feels he looks silly.

Now you're saying to yourself, "What kind of a guy would play these kinds of tricks?"

That's a judgment.

You are judging him. And since it's impossible to see things in someone that don't exist in us, we are judging ourselves.

Wouldn't it make more sense to accept him as he is? Then, we would be accepting ourselves, which is a giant step toward loving ourselves—which is the final step toward loving others.

30

WHO'S THE IDIOT? WE ALL ARE.

I'm sure that many times in your life you've said to yourself, "That man is an idiot."

Well, you know, like attracts like. It's like a magnet. We attract to ourselves the very thing we are suppressing.

And the thing we are suppressing yearns to be brought into the light, where it can be part of our whole being, not just shoved into some dark corner.

So up pops a man in our life who does idiotic things that remind us of the "idiot" we have suppressed. So, our idiot is brought to the light. Because we now think, "Hey I'm not the only one."

I'm not the only one who
burns the toast . . .
locks my keys in the car . . .
forgets appointments . . .

takes the wrong turn . . .

forgets an anniversary . . .

Suppressing is depressing. It's saying you have something to hide. Do you really want to tie yourself in knots over some minor mistakes? No. Neither does your neighbor.

I wonder if there is a way to rid ourselves of dark places to hide.

Then, with no place to hide, everything would be forced to remain in the light. Where it belongs.

31

ALLOW YOURSELF TO BE WRONG.

Do we want to be right or do we want peace?

Let's say you are in the midst of an argument or confrontation and can't find a way out. There is always the obvious—allow yourself to be wrong.

I was in a car with a friend of mine, driving from Chester, Pennsylvania to Philadelphia, when a statement was made by one of us that the other disagreed with. I'll never forget this experience. We were shouting at the top of our lungs. *It was! It wasn't! She did! She didn't!* Screaming as loud as we could scream. Then . . .

I was ready to scream again when all at once I realized he was right. And I said, "You know, you're right."

You could have heard a pin drop.

And then there was uproarious laughter after the silence. By both of us.

I had allowed myself to be wrong. And I felt good about it.

You don't have to be right to feel good.

32

WE'RE HERE TO GO FORWARD.

That doesn't mean building bigger buildings, weapons, cars, computers, etc. What it means is going forward in spirituality.

Sacrificing spirituality for technology is a serious misjudgment. Our purpose on earth has nothing to do with the products technology produces, other than how spirituality might be in alignment with them.

We're here to build a life that puts us on a path to God—giving, receiving, forgiving, praying, meditating, and sharing. These are some of the actions that reveal the path so that we can follow it. The path can be followed in your home, in a forest, on the beach, in jail, or in church. It doesn't matter where. Your soul goes with you wherever your travels take you. And removing the blockage that is obscuring our souls is the spiritual journey. That's how we go forward.

33

THE WORLD IS YOUR MIRROR. WHAT YOU SEE IS WHO YOU ARE.

I love to look at my personal movie because my viewpoint is different from any other person's, as is yours. It gives me an insight into what kind of thoughts I've been thinking and what kind of feelings they translate into. These thoughts and feelings manifest in the physical, creating your life.

Is your life exactly what you would like it to be? No? You have the power to change it.

Go inside, meditate. The stillness will help you see things more clearly. It's a way of healing. A way to bring thoughts of harmony and love to the surface.

Now, take a look at your life. Is it still the same?

Shakespeare said, "There is nothing either good or bad, but thinking makes it so."

BE THE PERSON YOU MOST WANT TO BE.

Do you want to emulate Muhammed Ali? Do you want to emulate Shakespeare? Do you want to emulate Leonardo DaVinci? Or, maybe you want to emulate Leonardo DiCaprio. Or, do your thoughts go to Mother Teresa or Jesus or Buddha or Mohammed?

Who is the person you most want to be? Most likely none of the above. I think most of us want to be our own person.

Only you know the answer.

So, dive deep down within yourself, seeking the stillness that allows your heart to release the one dynamic that defines your hidden desire. Whatever it may be. And you find that the dynamic, when released, is simply to go gently down the stream, meaning, without harm to anyone. So, no matter what your profession or vocation, you go through life as a loving, healing, giving soul.

35

KEEP STILL ABOUT THE KIND OF LIFE YOU DESIRE TO CREATE FOR YOURSELF.

Read my lips: Don't tell your intentions to other people. They won't understand. Only you know the full significance of your dream.

Somehow the idea loses it explosiveness when shared with others.

Human nature drives them to question the validity of someone else's plans. How can it work? They will say, "Where did you get such an idea?"

By revealing your goal, you're put into a position of having to defend it. The ego is clapping his hands. He loves to see aspirations chopped down. There will be no success if the ego can help it. No matter what you achieve, the ego sees to it that you are not satisfied.

So don't look for validation from the masses. Just quietly go forward.

Gandhi wrote, "Strength in numbers is the delight of the timid. The valiant in spirit glory in fighting alone."

Alone—there's a key word.

Can you imagine Einstein, DaVinci, or Copernicus explaining what they were working on, to friends and acquaintances? No way. They knew it would only lead to disparagement and humiliation.

Don't look for the approval of others, you take a charge out of the idea.

There it is again—silence is golden.

36

IF YOU ARE IN AN INSIDIOUS ROMANCE WITH THE EGO, BREAK OUT OF IT.

For those who are not familiar with the role the ego plays in everyone's life, it is the role of Satan, the enemy of God. Although to use the word enemy is to suggest that God could be overcome, which is a complete untruth.

The reason I say "enemy" is to get across the idea that Satan's influence would be in direct opposition to God's.

Think about your life. Do you go through the day making sure that each and every action is made with your protection in mind? The ego says, "Pull in your energy. Don't let anyone get close. Do it to him before he does it to you. Make sure you get the best of the deal. Don't say you broke the dish when nobody knows who did it. If they give the wrong change, and it favors you, keep it. Give your child the biggest piece of cake." And on and on and on.

The ego is a powerful presence. So, even though you do none

of these things and are very careful to be fair, the ego will work his black magic insidiously.

It is imperative to be vigilant to search ourselves every day for signs that we may be slipping away from the light.

37

IT'S IMPORTANT TO KNOW THAT FEAR EXPRESSING ITSELF IS ANGER, ABUSE, DISEASE, PAIN, GREED, ADDICTION, SELFISHNESS, OBSESSION, AND VIOLENCE.

Fear is the tool of the ego, and the ego will throw in your path all the negativity it can muster to knock you off your journey to the light.

I sometimes take a look at my life as if I'm watching a movie and try to see which of the emotional downers I have saddled myself with. If I discover any of the above, I know that fear is at the bottom of it.

Take a look at your life. If you see any of the above, know that it is in your power to change things. Because you control your thoughts. And your thoughts create your life.

WE MUST BE SERVING.

Find a quiet place to reflect and ask yourself, "Am I serving?"
No one is truly alive who is not in service to others.

The following prayer by Saint Francis of Assisi goes straight to
the heart:

Lord make me an instrument of thy peace
Where there is hatred let me sow Love
Where there is injury, Pardon
Where there is doubt, Faith
Where there is despair, Hope
Where there is darkness, Light
Where there is sadness, Joy
Divine Master; Grant that I may not so much
seek to be consoled as to Console
To be understood, as to Understand
To be loved as to Love
for it is in giving that we receive.

In pardoning that we are pardoned

And it is in dying that we are born to eternal life.

Now that you've read the prayer, ask yourself, "Do I seek to understand instead of only wanting to be understood?"

I look at each part of the prayer and ask myself, "Am I in partnership with this prayer of service?"

From my heart I say . . . find a way to serve.

HEAL YOUR NEIGHBOR
AND BE HEALED.

Of course you can't really heal your neighbor, you can only awaken the healing instrument within.

Sometimes just a touch on the shoulder will send a healing current through the body that carries a message to every cell: "Wake up—wake up." Doctors are only now awakening to this truth.

When we make an attempt to help a person heal himself, we are sending that message through our own bodies as well, to the exact degree.

"Do unto others as you would have them do unto you."

It means that when you do unto others, you are simultaneously doing unto yourself. Every time, without exception. It is a Law of the Universe.

Helping to heal is to heal yourself. If you accept this as truth, wouldn't it make sense to go on a crusade of healing to ease the pain of those in need?

I certainly think so.

40

WE ALL HAVE A MISSION IN LIFE, AND IF WE ARE STILL ALIVE ON THE PLANET, WE HAVEN'T ACCOMPLISHED IT.

I can remember being ready to step out into traffic on a very busy thoroughfare in Columbus, Ohio, when somebody grabbed my collar from behind and pulled me back.

He saved my life.

I recall very vividly, on the Jersey Shore, being yanked from the water by my father, who said that I was being pulled into the ocean by the strong undertow.

He saved my life.

In Western New York, on a road that appeared to be clear and dry, I hit glare ice, spun out of control, hit an embankment and turned over twice. I walked away without a scratch.

My life was saved—somehow.

In Niagara Falls, New York, on a severely cold day, after a day of rain and snow, I was driving over a small bridge that turned out to be very slippery. Again, I went out of control and rammed into a guardrail. As I sat there collecting myself, I was slammed by a jack-knifing semi, which did enormous damage to the car. I walked away completely intact.

One thing is clear. My mission on earth has yet to be accomplished.

41

LOVE EXPRESSING ITSELF IS KINDNESS, GIVING, MERCY, COMPASSION, PEACE, JOY, ACCEPTANCE, JOINING, AND NON-JUDGMENT.

Now . . . you are a person filled with the Love of the Universe.

Act on any desire you have. Love will be your partner. Success will be in the cards, because fear is not your companion.

Put all of the qualities of love expressing itself in a pot. Add a measure of universal energy to the mixture. Mentally stir for only one second. And you have God's recipe for divine harmony. Sip and digest slowly for best results.

KNOW THAT BENEATH THE SURFACE OF EVERY ABUSIVE ACT IS A CRY FOR HELP.

This is a difficult one because it hits us in so many ways, every day of our lives.

And that thought is *to know that beneath the surface of every abusive act is a cry for help.*

If we could only look at life as if it were a movie that clearly shows the insecurity of the perpetrator, we would understand his cry for help.

Of all the books I have read, all the lectures I've attended, all the tapes I've listened to, one piece of advice lingers in my thoughts like no other. Every fit of anger, every show of arrogance, every act of hostility, all insensitivity, and every act of violence should be viewed as a call for help. View them all as a call for help. A call for understanding.

Because beneath the surface of all who are being abusive, or acting hostile, or showing anger, is a fearful, overburdened, painful, stressed out, tired, and, yes, insecure personality, crying out for help.

We've all been there.

Looking back in our lives, we can all remember a time when we would have liked to cry out, "Please understand me. This is not the real me you're seeing. Underneath I am a kind, caring, loving, individual."

43

TAKE CARE OF THE OTHER GUY, AND GOD WILL TAKE CARE OF YOU.

Everyone wants to be happy. But can you be happy if those around you are in despair? Of course not. There was a song in which these lyrics stated a way to happiness is giving joy to the other guy.

The composer of that song must have been thinking the above thought. Take care of the other guy, and God will take care of you.

And there's no question about it. It's like Catch 22, though we have to love ourselves first. It's good to put the focus on the other guy. Make sure he is comfortable. Do as much as possible to enhance the quality of his life.

Give to the needy. Whether that means money to a desperate person or even support of another kind of desperation.

44

> ## A GOOD TREE CANNOT BEAR BAD FRUIT, AND A BAD TREE CANNOT BEAR GOOD FRUIT.
> —MATTHEW 7:18

A Good Tree

Intention comes from within.

If your intention is to be loving,
If your intention is to be giving,
If your intention is to be non-judgmental,
If your intention is to be Godly . . .

then, it is *impossible* to portray any lesser quality in the physical. Your physical life will reflect those qualities I have listed.

45

DO YOUR BEST AND YOU PASS THE TEST.

Give it your all, and you'll stand tall.

Whatever field of endeavor you have chosen.

Whatever sport you are playing.

Whether you cook the food,

or wash the dishes.

Whether it's running,

or sewing,

or rowing,

or mowing.

Give it your best, and you pass the test.

Doing your best negates guilt.

It's only when you don't give your all that you feel guilty.

You don't have to be "the" best.

Just do your best.

Then no one can judge you, because you did your best.

Go through one day of doing your best.

Then go through another day of doing your best.

Soon, you'll realize that things are getting done, and you feel better about yourself. It won't be long before doing your best will become a habit, and you'll find yourself walking tall.

And you'll love it.

46

HELP THOSE WHO NEED HELP, AND YOU'LL BE HELPING YOURSELF TO THE EXACT DEGREE.

One cold night in Manhattan, I was wandering around and came across a couple putting a blanket on a homeless man who was sleeping on the street with a piece of cardboard for a bed. Then, they placed a bag of food under the blanket.

That's giving without seeking a return. Those people had open hearts. They took the time to help another human being, without asking who and where he was from. Their only thought was to make him more comfortable, without seeking approval.

Those people will be rewarded.

Somehow.

47

THERE IS NO SUCH THING AS FAILURE.

Failure suggests an ending. There are no endings. It's saying to ourselves, "There are no more options." Certainly there are more options. "Time has run out." Time never runs out. "We've reached the end of the line." Not true.

There is always a possible solution, another combination of ingredients that will produce the desired results.

The only ending would be death, which isn't an ending at all, but a transition and a new beginning.

And if taken in the context of only this expression of life, the desired result is always there. It's only a matter of changing the recipe and carrying on. The cake will eventually arrive. With all the trimmings.

I couldn't bake a cake if my life depended on it. But looking back, I see that I have been able to bake a couple of symbolic cakes and hope for more in the future.

And of course, the truth of the matter is that if I continued trying to really bake a cake, eventually a wonderful, succulent chocolate cake would materialize—as it would for everyone.

So, *there is no such thing as failure* belongs on the list of thoughts that lead to happiness because holding on to that thought eliminates anxiety and worry, and brings a positive flow of energy, which increases the ability to succeed.

Success comes from trial and error, and it seems to me that happiness is found in the quest to attain, not so much in the actual achievement.

If at first you don't succeed, try, try, again.

Whoever said that was saying there is no such thing as failure.

48

USE EVERY AVENUE OPEN TO YOU IN ORDER TO REACH YOUR GOAL, YOUR DREAM.

In other words, don't leave any stone unturned. It is important for the universe to know that your intention is to succeed and that you are doing your best to make that success occur.

Colonel Sanders knocked and knocked and knocked until someone finally accepted his fried chicken recipe. He had climbed his personal mountain and came face to face with his dream, a huge chain of Kentucky Fried Chicken restaurants.

49

REVEAL YOURSELF.

I was sitting in a circle of three at a metaphysical seminar in north Georgia. The assignment was to meditate for five minutes and then tell the other two what you experienced.

After the other two spoke of their experiences, they asked me what I got.

"Nothing," I said. "I just didn't get anything—at least anything worth mentioning."

"Well then you did get something. What was it?"

"Okay, I got 'reveal yourself'!"

You could feel the hush in the room when I said those words.

The teacher of the class came running over and said, "Did you say 'reveal yourself'? You could write a book on it," she said.

Now, as I think of revealing yourself, I can see that, as you reveal yourself, you become aware of powerful truths that were formerly hidden because of the blockage of the flow caused by the baggage crammed inside, which was finally revealed.

I can see now that to reveal is to no longer be living in dark corners, that a healthy body goes along with a healthy revelation.

I could actually say "reveal yourself and be free."

50

OPEN YOUR HEART AND ALLOW YOURSELF TO FEEL THE JOY OF LIVING.

It happened in the auditorium of my daughter's grade school. It was an unusual year in that the annual school play was performed by the sixth grade—not the senior class, which is customary.

My daughter was in the play that year—she has a wonderful voice. My wife and I were in the audience, and I can tell you my heart was wide open that night, because I love my daughter, and I share her enthusiasm for the theatrical.

So when she stepped up to do her solo song, I can only say that I was overwhelmed with emotion stemming from her complete confidence and her wonderful rendition.

I was consumed with sobbing. My heart was open, and as I looked around the audience I saw that I wasn't the only one with an open heart. It was an evening I'll never forget.

51

EVERYTHING IS POSSIBLE FOR HIM WHO BELIEVES.

When I opened my carpet store in Key West, Florida, I was thrilled to have my own business. Although it was tiny, I felt an emotional high I had never before experienced.

I knew that I could make it in that business.

I'll go even further. A voice inside told me, "This is the opportunity you've been waiting for." I didn't actually hear the voice. It was more like a truth being pressed into me. Somehow, I knew. And guess what? That little business grew to be the dominant carpet store of the Florida Keys.

When you *feel*, when you *believe*, when you know, the possibilities are endless.

TO THE EXTENT THAT YOU FIND POSSIBLE, BANISH FEAR FROM YOUR LIFE.

In so doing, love will fill the void. At once. Love surrounds us. It's as if you jumped into a swimming pool. The water would surround you. Love is with us in that very way. The problem is, negativity gets in the way.

Have you ever thought about a pegboard of negativity? Fear, Jealousy, Greed, Resentment, Anger, Doubt, Hostility—all have separate pegs. Now, suppose you could find a way to never be jealous again. The jealousy peg would be pulled from the board, and love would fill the void immediately, and you would become a more loving person. As the pegs are removed, the more loving a person you become and the more your life changes. You'll be thinking, "Boy, I feel good."

Of course, love is having its way.

53

KNOW THAT YOUR BODY IS YOUR TEMPLE.

How do you reach the inner sanctuary? Simply close your eyes. Try it. No matter where you are or what you are doing, closing your eyes brings on the awareness of your temple. Can't you feel the peaceful silence? It's impossible not to.

When you close the eyelids, you shut yourself off from the outside world, and with a few deep breaths you can relax in the splendor of your inner life.

After all, one of the main functions of the eyelids is to allow your eyes to feed information in where the work is done. This feeding is done along with the other four senses. That's what the five senses do. They feed information in to be processed so you can function in the physical world.

You are Spirit. Retreat into your temple.

LOVE WITHOUT THE ANXIETY OF WHETHER OR NOT YOUR LOVE WILL BE RETURNED.

That's the secret of getting closer to God. There's a universal flow of energy, a divine energy, that is eternal in its essence. Loving with no conditions puts you in the flow. When you put conditions on your love, you block your entrance to the flow, as if you were rowing upstream against a strong current. It's important to give your love and keep giving so that you keep moving in the same direction, towards God.

55

ALL PRAYERS ARE ANSWERED IN SOME WAY, SOMEHOW.

I can't put too much emphasis on how important it is to you to either pray or meditate every day. Or both.

Without some contact with Spirit, your entire inner life is put on hold, and you exist strictly in the physical. Plus, you are denying the existence of your soul, and your soul is pure love. Why in the world would you not want to be in contact with your soul as much as possible? It has so much to do with answering prayers.

By living only in the physical, you miss the help that is offered to you by your divine essence, because you are not tuned in.

Do yourself a huge favor. Pray every day.

FOCUS ON WHAT YOU WANT, NOT WHAT YOU DON'T WANT.

When I was eight years old, a thought came to me: what a wonderful thing to be able to live your life near water.

I was living in Newark, New Jersey, as was most of my family until some of them moved to the Jersey shore. That was okay with me, because each summer they would invite me to visit them, and I would spend most of the summer there. Upon reflection, I realize those were quite happy days in my life. The beach, the ocean, and the boardwalk. I loved them all.

The dream of living near the water stayed with me through the years. The focus had never left my mind. Not that I was consciously thinking about it. Somehow, it was just there.

It was about thirty years later, when I was traveling around the country with a musical group, that we were booked in a club in Key West, Florida, an island off the mainland of Florida. I didn't leave until thirty years later. Of course, I still maintain a home there.

Even now, my new home is located on a lake in Western New York.

I certainly got what I focused on. Of course, we always get what we focus on. We're just not aware of it.

Make sure you focus on what you want, not what you don't want.

It's a step toward happiness.

57

SHARE YOUR LIFE.

I mean truly share your life. I don't know why I am including this thought in this book, because sharing my life is one of my biggest problems. I tend to hide behind an invisible wall that nobody knows is there except me. We might be exchanging personal ideas and you all at once reach out with a friendly gesture and run smack into the wall of cold. That's what I call it. It's not always there, or I would be living in total isolation.

I truly find it difficult to share my life. Sharing your life means sharing on a soul level. Marc Gafni, in his book *Soul Prints*, calls this kind of sharing soul prints, the title of the book.

The gist of all this is that if you are not sharing your "soul prints," you are buried in loneliness.

It doesn't matter how involved you are in business, family, leisure. If you are not sharing from the soul level with a partner who picks up on it, you are stepping away from happiness.

I am constantly searching for the soul connection, mostly

through meditation. And when I sometimes get a glimpse of it, I simply feel better.

Are you coming from the soul with your partner for life? I hope so.

It's a gigantic step towards happiness.

58

STOP SAYING THE CREATOR OWES YOU BECAUSE HE BROUGHT YOU HERE.

The Creator owes you nothing. Yes, he is responsible for you having a life in the physical. But look at that as a blessing, not as God's obligation to guarantee your happiness.

The Creator has endowed you with the tools to bring to yourself anything you desire in life. I mean *Anything You Desire In Life*.

There is one rule that must be followed. It is imperative to have love in your heart. Then, anything is possible. Health and wealth will be yours with hardly a finger lifted. You will find that all goals are reachable, because love knows no boundaries.

Use the tool of love to manifest your dreams. You don't need God to do it. You have a Divine Presence.

You do it.

59

TRUST.

It was the tiniest of carpet stores, with a minimum of inventory. I had given a hundred dollars to the landlord for the first month's rent, which left me with just a hundred dollars. Although it was a very small space, even a small space seems cavernous when there is nothing to fill it. I would spend the hundred dollars on inventory.

"Small remnants are what I need, and Miami is the place to find them," I thought. So, I took the three and one-half hour drive and managed to find a carpet retailer called Surplus Carpet.

I sought out the owner and explained the situation. He immediately pointed to a loft and said "Go up that ladder. I think what you want is up there."

Following his instructions, up the ladder I went to find hundreds of carpet remnants. All sizes, colors, and textures.

I told the dealer "Here is a hundred dollars. Please send me what you consider a hundred dollars' worth to be. To my surprise and joy, he agreed and took the money.

"Give me three or four days," he said.

Three days later, a delivery truck rolled up in front of my shop with a cargo of fifty carpet remnants all sizes and colors—all bound on four sides with matching tape.

It turned out I had paid two dollars each. I was amazed.

I trusted him, and he came through like a champion.

Trust eliminates anxiety.

Trust eliminates tension.

Trust eliminates stress.

When you trust, you can relax—a thought that definitely leads to happiness.

60

GIVE WITHOUT THE EXPECTATION OF RETURN.

There are many ways of giving.

Give money to a person or a charity who needs it.

Give love to a desperate person.

Give clothing to a threadbare soul.

Give time to someone who needs to tell her story.

The list goes on and on.

Then there are the simple day-to-day ways of giving, like the time I was standing in a line at the supermarket. There I was with an overloaded cart, third in line. And there was an elderly lady with two items in her hand. It seemed like the thing to do was trade places. She thanked me and I took her place at the end of the line. No sooner did I reach the back of the line when a cashier called me to an aisle that she was opening up. To my surprise, I was now first in line.

I'm sure something similar has happened to you at one time or another. It's just another way of giving without seeking a return. Sometimes karma works instantly.

Giving is going with the flow.

Expecting a return is looking for something to buck the flow of positive energy. It is operating with the future in mind, thus allowing worry to enter the scenario.

Stay in the present.

Give, and have it stop there.

You take a giant step towards happiness.

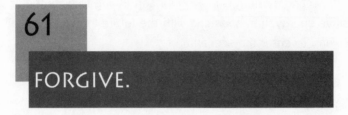

61

FORGIVE.

Nothing is more important in a person's life than to allow forgiveness to be in the forefront.

When you choose to forgive everyone for anything you perceive may have been done to you, your heart is relieved of the burden of carrying grudges, which demand enormous energy. Then a loving mindset is put in motion that knows no boundaries.

Everyone wants to find a way to become one with the peace and serenity that lies within. Forgiving puts you right there.

When you forgive, you are forgiven.

Simultaneously. You don't have to do anything else.

You are free.

A great step towards happiness has been taken.

62

WE ARE ALL EXAMPLES OF THE PRODIGAL SON LIVING IN A FAR COUNTRY.

In most religions, the question "Are you a God-fearing man?" is asked. They take for granted that if you are not a God-fearing man, somehow you are lacking something, that it is a given that fear is in every scenario where God is concerned.

In my opinion, "Are you an ego-fearing man?" would make more sense to ask.

What is there to fear about God?

God is love. Total love.

No matter how we behave.

No matter what so-called sins have been committed, God has always welcomed back into his fold anyone seeking his love. Just as he welcomed back the Bible's prodigal son and proceeded to throw a party for him.

God is about love.

God is not about fear.

Call on God and take a step toward happiness.

63

STOP TRYING TO BE THE TOP ONE.

Kris Kristofferson and Barbra Streisand were singing "Evergreen" in the film *A Star Is Born*. As I watched the movie on TV, I was overcome by the sheer talent of these people. It was like a thunderbolt had struck my heart, causing an emotional outburst. My heart was wide open.

Sometimes, when your heart has been opened, things get through to you that wouldn't have if you were walking around with a closed heart.

In this case, a thought came through: "Stop trying to be the top one." Are you so sure some people are trying to take advantage of you? Maybe what they are saying is true.

Why not send them love instead of doubt of their honesty? Maybe you won't be on top, but you will be at peace. And so will the people you are dealing with.

64

WE ARE ALL WORTHY.

When I say worthy, I mean we are:

Worthy of Abundance . . .

Worthy of Peacefulness . . .

Worthy of Joy . . .

Worthy of Good Health . . .

Worthy of Loving Relationships . . .

Worthy of Manifesting Any Desire . . .

How could we not be Worthy?

We are Divine—All part of the same Spirit that exists in every man. The spirit that is God.

Oh, we're worthy, all right. As children we know it. Until adults teach another way of thinking. They have learned limitedness and foist it on their children unknowingly.

But just because they are swimming in limitations, does not mean they are unworthy. It just means they have lost contact with their inner power, the power that can manifest anything, anywhere, at any time.

We are worthy.

Do you think God would welcome back into his fold the prodigal son (meaning the entire human race) if he were unworthy? Beneath the facade of physicality is Divine Worthiness.

65

IF YOU'RE THINKING "I'LL NEVER AMOUNT TO ANYTHING," MY ADVICE TO YOU IS STOP SAYING "I'LL NEVER AMOUNT TO ANYTHING."

Stop saying, "I'm not smart enough."

Stop saying, "There isn't enough time."

Stop saying, "I don't know how."

Stop saying, "I'm short of money."

Stop saying, "Nobody loves me."

Stop saying, "I'm a failure."

Stop saying, "I'm always sick."

Stop saying, "I'm powerless."

Stop saying, "I can't even find a girl/boy friend."

Stop saying, "I'm afraid I'll fail."

Stop feeling you're always wrong.

Stop, Stop, Stop, Stop, Stop, Stop, Stop—and . . .

Start saying, "With God as my companion, I can do anything."

Start saying, "I feel really good."

Start saying, "What a beautiful day."

Start saying, "I give thanks for all I have."

Start saying, "I hope all my friends become successful."

Start saying, "I can face any problem, knowing I'll move through it."

Start saying, "I love you."

Keep saying, "I love you."

Start saying, "I am calm, relaxed, at peace, and in love."

Start saying, "I don't believe in failure."

Start being gracious, kind, and considerate.

Start caring.

Start sharing.

Your life will change for the better.

66

AN ISOLATED HAPPENING CAN BRING SIGNIFICANT INSIGHTS.

One afternoon after a heavy downpour, my wife, Emmy, and I were driving east on South Roosevelt Boulevard in Key West, Florida, when I said, "Look at that beautiful rainbow." Only a few seconds later, as we went around a bend, we ran smack into the end of the rainbow. It came right into the car.

Nothing like that had ever happened to us before.

Later, I said to myself, "There must be more to this than meets the eye. What is the universe trying to tell us?"

A rainbow right in my car? This has to be one in a million.

And then I started thinking, "What's proverbially at the end of a rainbow is the Pot of Gold."

In this case, we were the Pot of Gold.

"Does that make sense?" I asked myself.

In other words, we don't need a Pot of Gold. We are the Pot of Gold.

Being Divine, we can manifest any desire we have if we make thought and feeling one with the desire.

(Please don't say "Are we back to that Divine business again?")

We are Divine—and we can manifest—who do you think put the thought and feeling into what has been manifested in your life so far? You did.

That rainbow was saying to us, "You have the power—*go for it!*"

EVERY LIFE IS IMPORTANT, AND EVERY LIFE AFFECTS WHAT IS AROUND IT.

In the film, *It's A Wonderful Life*, this thought is perfectly depicted.

If you remember, George loses eight thousand dollars, or at least blames himself for the whole set of circumstances that occur because the money is gone.

And because he is beside himself with worry and guilt, he cries to his personal angel, (who was sent down from heaven to help him) "I wish I was never born."

Clarence, who is trying to win permanent angel wings, thought, "This is perfect. I'll show him the Bedford Falls that would exist if he had never been born." (In other words, he was shown an alternate world.)

So, George's wish is granted. He gets to see Bedford Falls without the energy he had brought to it.

It wasn't pretty.

People who were friendly, loving, and kind were now angry, hostile, and resentful.

The entire community was consumed with distrust, viciousness, and hatred.

It seemed George was the catalyst to bring love to the community, and since he had never been born, the love was missing.

Every person on earth is George, in one form or another.

EVERY ACTION IS THE BEGINNING OF A HABIT— SOMETIMES GOOD, SOMETIMES NOT SO GOOD.

Like the time I decided to go for a drive at 1:00 A.M. While driving around, I came across an all-night donut shop. (I am not supposed to eat any sweets.) "What can it hurt," I said to myself, "One donut and some coffee?" Just a plain donut with none of the sugar coating. So, I went in and got my donut and coffee.

And the next night, what did I do? Right. Another drive and another treat of donut and coffee. And on and on until I finally stopped it.

And what about the time I swore off gambling and went into an off-track betting parlor just to watch. No way! The temptation is too great. It's just another donut story.

And then, there's the time I finally started putting the toilet seat down. This was great. I got a reward from my wife every time I did it. She didn't say a word. As I said earlier, silence is certainly golden.

69

TRY THIS: SAY TO YOURSELF,
"WHEN I AWAKEN IN THE
MORNING, I AM GOING TO
GIVE THIS DAY TO GOD."

Now, when you do this also say to yourself, "I am just going to go through the day, merely breezing along—doing what I usually do—but with no anxiety attached. Nothing to worry about—God is in my corner."

See if you aren't better off, or at least just as well off than if you had gone through your normal day with all the anxiousness and fear attached to it.

When you give the day to God, in essence you are saying, "I allow the day to unfold as God sees fit." Then, continuing for an unspecified number of days, the Universe will begin to reveal to you paths to follow that will draw you closer to your destiny, because they come straight from the Universe—God's Universe.

70

BE INFINITELY PATIENT.

In one of my earlier thoughts, I mention that if you cut yourself you have absolute confidence in the body's ability to heal itself.

Confidence could not show itself if infinite patience did not come right along with it.

I love the line by Shakespeare: "How poor are they that have not patience! What wound did ever heal but by degree?"

Wayne Dyer, in his book *Wisdom of the Ages*, quotes a passage out of *A Course in Miracles*. The line reads, "Infinite Patience produces immediate results." Yes. Yes.

Because Infinite Patience is a sign of entering the world of the eternal. It is saying that you know the expected result will be forthcoming, that a connection has been made that draws the impetus ever closer to the result.

71

ALLOW NATURE TO BE A HEALING FACTOR IN YOUR LIFE.

It all began with the suggestion to a chiropractor that an artificial spine be placed on the desk of a person who suffers from scoliosis. Seeing the straight spine would have a straightening effect on her own spine.

Then it came to me that, since inside us is a counterpart to everything in nature, wouldn't it make sense to walk in the woods, open to the idea that seeing the perfection of nature would have a medicinal effect on whatever part of our body coincides with what we were viewing in the woods? I use the woods only as an example. It could be Niagara Falls, the Pacific Ocean, Mt. Rainier, etc.

The main thing is to have in mind the healing effect of whatever you have come to view.

Absorbing, via the five senses, and sending the message inside where the work is done, cannot help but bring positive effects. *After all, it is pure Divine Energy.*

THERE ARE NO COINCIDENCES.

There I was, going from job to job—sometimes in music, sometimes in shoes, sometimes in furniture.

Then my father entered the Spirit world.

Shortly thereafter, I opened a carpet store on very, very little money.

Did my father have something to do with it? It's pretty well documented that the Spirit world helps those still in the physical.

The landlord's girlfriend was originally supposed to be part of the project, but dropped out for reasons unknown.

Did my father have something to do with that? I was better off without a partner.

The business flourished and I bought real estate that skyrocketed in value.

Did my father have something to do with that?

Some people might say it was just a coincidence.

Personally, I don't think so.

There are no coincidences.
My father was there.

73

ASK FOR WHAT YOU WANT—YOU MIGHT GET IT.

In our jobs, in our relationships, in any aspect of our lives, we so often don't come clean and ask for what we want.

In July of 1951, I was sitting on Virginia Beach, with a radio by my side, when I heard the draft had been reactivated. I said to my companion, "I'll be in the army in six months." I was.

But the night before I was to report, a friend who had served during WWII gave me a piece of advice: don't listen to everybody and keep your mouth shut—ask for what you want, you might get it.

So after basic training and a few weeks in cook school, I ended up in clerk typist school.

After graduating (four weeks), we were interviewed for which assignment we would get. I thought that was strange; why not just send us?

Anyway, when my turn came, the Major said they had an opening in Fort Meade, Maryland, which was not far from Pennsylvania, my home at the time.

"I'll take it," I said.

"You'll have to pull KP (kitchen police) and go out in the field," he said.

"No thanks," I said.

"What do you want?" he asked.

"I want to go to Valley Forge Army Hospital." Actually, I thought I had about a 1 percent chance.

"Wait outside," he said.

When he was through interviewing, he came up to me and said, "Now you want to go to VFAH?"

"Right," I said.

"Wait a minute," he said.

About three minutes later, he returned and said, "Don't worry, you're going to VFAH. Here are your papers."

Valley Forge was a terrific post to serve your time in the army. My friend was right. Ask and you shall receive.

ROW, ROW, ROW YOUR BOAT, GENTLY DOWN THE STREAM. MERRILY, MERRILY, MERRILY, MERRILY LIFE IS BUT A DREAM.

It was at a seminar of Shirley MacLaine's that I had a wonderful experience.

During a break, I approached Ms. MacLaine and asked, "Have you heard the song *Row, Row, Row Your Boat?*"

"Of course," she said, "Hasn't everybody?"

"But have you thought about the lyrics."

"No, what about them," she inquired.

"Think about it," I said. "The composer said 'row' three times—in other words, he meant it. Get moving."

"But do it gently. Gently is defined in *A Course in Miracles* as meaning, 'without harm.'"

"Down the stream—with the flow of Universal energy. With the flow of consciousness."

"Merrily, merrily, merrily, merrily, four times. He's saying 'be joyful.'"

"Life is but a dream." And each of us has our own individual dream.

At the end of the seminar Shirley had 700 people holding hands singing, *Row, Row, Row Your Boat*.

75

YOUR SOUL GLOWS WITH EVERLASTING BRIGHTNESS. IT IS THE TRUE YOU.

I'm saying that the glow of a soul will outshine any physical presence; of course, why not? The soul is spiritual and timeless, and when uncovered, shines with a brightness not to be found in the physical world.

Your true being is not your physical body. But rather your all-loving soul. And when your become aware of and uncover the loving soul you will outshine every star.

That's the spiritual path.

76

CONFRONT THE PROBLEM, AND RESOLVE IT.

There is so much power in confronting the issue and so much peacefulness awaiting you at the other end.

I can remember so vividly the day a customer of mine walked in the door of my carpet shop and said, "My carpet is absolutely flat."

Now, I knew that nine other couples had bought the same style, which amounted to more than 1000 yards of carpeting.

I had a choice. Dodge the issue by using any number of excuses to deny replacement, or confront the issue and attempt to resolve it.

I chose the latter.

I went to see the carpet. It was flat. I replaced it.

The nine other couples showed up.

I replaced all of those carpets.

There were two carpet companies involved. One replaced what they had sold me and the other refused to.

The making good on our promise to satisfy the customer so early in the life of the business was the key to the great success of the business.

I confronted the issue.

Oh, yeah—ten years later, at the market in Atlanta, I walked into the space of the company that refused to make good.

I said to the owner, "You have nice carpet, but I wouldn't buy a square inch."

"Why not?" he asked.

So I related the story that had happened ten years prior.

He looked at me and said, "Wait here. Don't leave."

When he returned, he handed me a credit for the carpeting I had lost.

The peacefulness consumed me.

77

LOVE IS THE VEHICLE TO SUCCESS.

I am always awestruck by the talent, the insight, the glowing thoughts of the authors, poets, composers, and playwrights who have written marvelous lines that urge us to take a good look at ourselves. It's almost a demand. You read them, and you can't help but think, "Is that true of me?"

In thousands of songs they write of love as being the vehicle to success in life.

It's a powerful statement of fact.

Since love equates with nature and finally with God, there is no doubt when you have love you *will* make it.

And you will be able to give love because it takes having love to be able to give love. And that's what's important.

78

BE CAREFUL NOT TO CREATE FALSE IMAGES IN YOUR MIND.

Only a few days ago, I had an experience which showed that is exactly what I did. I created a false image.

I was about to purchase a building, and in so doing, was asked by the seller to sign a letter of intention before the closing date. He asked if I would mind using the same lawyer (his) and share the expenses. He said the document was nothing to worry about, and would I come over and sign it to get it out of the way. I began to feel a little uneasy.

I must say that I have the utmost admiration for this man, who is open, forthright, and honest.

Yet, over the next few days, I built up in my mind an image of a man trying to take advantage of me using his guile to get me to sign a paper without having my lawyer look it over.

By the time I got to his office, I can tell you my image of him wasn't very good.

But upon seeing him again, I was astonished at how absolutely wrong I was about him. I had temporarily lost my feelings of love and trust.

79

BE NOT DOMINATED BY APPEARANCES. THEN YOU WILL NOT BE REACTING—YOU WILL BE INITIATING.

A while back, I was talking to a man who told me that it wasn't long ago that he was desperate for attention and conversation. He felt that he had let himself become too heavy, and that was the reason he had trouble relating.

He would go out in the evening with this intense desire to meet people, with desperation written all over him. It's not the energy people are likely to pick up on.

So, it just didn't happen for him—until he came to the conclusion that it wasn't his appearance hampering him, it was his focusing on a specific outcome.

Instead of going out looking for something, he realized, a better way would be just going out and letting the chips fall where they may.

He said things have been better lately.

80

ADRENALINE IS GOD'S MAGIC ELIXIR. IT ALLOWS PEOPLE TO RISE ABOVE THEIR EVERYDAY ABILITIES WHEN THE NEED ARISES.

I guess everybody has heard the story about the man who lifted the side of a car to free someone. God's magic elixir gave him that strength.

I can remember a rather comical occurrence when adrenaline came into play.

It seems there was to be an auction of appliances in a nearby city. Joe had twelve small refrigerators to put up for auction, and for some reason was late loading the truck. When they finally got started, the three men he had hired to load the refrigerators on the truck were struggling.

Time was passing. He was afraid the auction would be over.

Suddenly he pushed the three men aside and said, "Look. Do it like this!"

He proceeded to single-handedly load the refrigerators, using strength that had to come straight from God. Adrenaline had kicked in.

IN ALL TRANSACTIONS AND ALL OF LIFE'S ACTIVITIES, MAKE SURE THEY ARE COMPLETED WITH THE GOOD OF EVERYONE CONCERNED.

Don't let a rosy-looking short-run gain influence you into making a deal that is obviously not in the best interests of the other person.

Because, it is, without doubt, not in your best interest. It is clouding the circumstances, so the other guy doesn't understand the full impact of the deal.

In a way, it is bearing false witness.

It is setting yourself up to be smacked down later.

It is going against the flow and introduces worry and fear into the equation, and leaves love far behind.

It is not doing what you know is the right thing.

The short-term abundance that you maneuvered will surely negate any long-term abundance that was flowing toward you.

82

WHEN THE STUDENT IS READY, THE TEACHER WILL APPEAR.

When I say this, I mean *not maybe, not sometimes*—in every case. It's a matter of awareness. Do you recognize the teacher when he arrives?

I could go a step further and say that life is a schoolroom. We are surrounded by teachers, moment to moment.

The guy who complained about the water from your roof running on to his property. He's a teacher—he's teaching property management.

The lady running after you with a broom because you are always leaving your garbage by the door instead of in the can provided.

She's a teacher.

She's teaching common courtesy.

The guy who knocked you down for touching his lady friend.

He's a teacher.

He's teaching good manners.

The grocer who called the cop on the beat because he saw you put candy in a bag you were carrying, and you obviously were not going to pay for it.

He's a teacher.

He's teaching one of the ten commandments: "Thou shalt not steal."

The list is endless—watch for the teachers as you go about your daily business.

83

ALLOW, ALLOW, ALLOW, ALLOW.

This is a thought that applies to you all day, every day. What's happening is that you are making choices pertaining to situations popping up all day long. A lot of them have to do with being angry.

For example:

I used to be annoyed every time a driver didn't follow the courtesy rules at a four-way stop.

I used to get angry when my wife didn't date the check stubs and didn't record the bank account balance.

It used to blow my mind when the movie suddenly stopped because of a malfunction.

I really became upset when somebody fumbled with their money at the register in the supermarket.

I used to climb up the walls when the pizza didn't arrive on time, when the alarm failed to go off, when the car wouldn't start, and when I forgot my keys to my shop.

I could go on and on and on.

Now, I just enter the universal flow of energy and allow things to unfold. It reduces the tension, and it reduces the stress.

I know I don't need that kind of anger and neither do you.

When you finally realize there is no need for all this anger, that it's just a choice after all, you will feel a great weight being lifted from your body.

84

STOP TRYING TO FORCE YOUR POINT OF VIEW ON OTHERS.

Let's face it. The more you force your point of view on others, the more resistance you meet. Escalate and the resistance builds.

Generally, people are too busy giving their point of view to take heed of yours.

You're just wasting your energy.

I like what Deepak Chopra said in his book, *The Seven Spiritual Laws of Success.*

Don't defend, and an argument won't start. Then, you fully experience the present, which is a gift.

That's why they call it the "present."

Then, you can say to yourself, "No more making my point of view the only one."

And with that statement, you have put yourself in line to start rowing downstream with the current and with joy in your heart.

It's true. Make the affirmation and watch what happens.

SEE THE MOVIE **CHOCOLAT**.

The movie is about a woman who opens a chocolate shop in a town that is badly in need of help.

It seems that Madame Chocolat has psychic powers and uses the power to dispense the correct chocolate to ease the burden of each individual customer.

One of the first was a plain-looking woman with an ordinary-looking husband.

Madame Chocolat sized up the situation and advised the woman to buy the chocolate that had aphrodisiacs.

She purchased the chocolate, which her husband partook of.

The next day, she was back for a double portion.

As each townsperson purchased her suggestion of chocolate, they found that negative situations in their lives cleared up.

Never did Madame Chocolat ask for anything in return except sometimes the price of the chocolate.

The end of the film shows her dreams coming true.

The moral? Give and be of service. It's a shortcut to God.

86

BEGIN.

When I opened my carpet store, although it was as small as small could be, it was a beginning.

To begin is to create an imaginary line between the beginning and the goal you have in mind.

When I opened up, I knew the goal I had in mind, but I didn't dwell on it. I began and did what I had to do to survive each day. My mind was on today's needs, not tomorrow's dreams.

How can you achieve anything if you don't simply begin? Because, to begin is to knock.

What's that line in the Bible?

"In the beginning . . . "

WE ARE SPIRITUAL BEINGS HAVING A HUMAN EXPERIENCE.

And in that journey we are reacquainting ourselves with who we really are.

If we accept that thought, aren't we unlimited in what we can manifest in the physical?

Do you realize we are manifesting our lives moment to moment?

Your life as you know it today didn't randomly happen. It is the result of your thoughts. Think back twenty-five years. At that time, could you have imagined that your life would be what it is today? Of course not. Do you think you arrived at where you are simply by reacting to outside forces? Do you think that your life will evolve to something better only if you get lucky with outside conditions? Nothing could be further from the truth.

We are all spiritual. We are all Divine. We control our destiny by our thoughts and feelings. The problem is, we've lost the focus. The solution is: Get it back. That's the spiritual journey.

88

IF YOU MEET A PERSON WHO IS IN ABSOLUTE DESPAIR, YOU COULD SAY TO HIM, "DO THIS NOW! BEGIN TO WORK ON BEING HUMBLE. REALLY WORK ON IT."

Next. Give, give, give. Your time, your energy in selflessness. And don't think about what you're going to get out of it. Just do it.

Then, be as loving as you know how. Do it now. Now. Now. In the present. Stay in the present. Stop dwelling on the past and future.

There is no way you won't feel better.

"Being humble" is another way of saying "allow." You allow things to happen around you without the controlling factor. There is no need to control, then there is a natural unimpeded flow of energy, bringing to you the life you deserve but were unable to experience because of fear (the need to control).

89

DO THE THING YOU CAN'T DO. STRETCH YOURSELF.

It happened during my junior year in high school.

I was playing softball in the city league. That day I was playing left field. I'll never forget it. The centerfielder was one of the best athletes my high school had known. He had graduated the year before.

Every ball that was hit anywhere between us, he would wave me off, then catch it.

Then, late in the game, a ball was hit with such power it looked like it either was going to go out of the park or hit the fence.

The centerfielder yelled to me, "Go get it." So I took off towards the fence. He had given up on it. As I was running, I noticed a small mound of dirt. I ran for it. When I reached it, I jumped as high as I could and threw my right arm up as high as I could, never even thinking I could reach the ball.

I had stretched my body as far as I could and, miracle of

miracles, the ball plopped in my glove. No one was as surprised as me.

I had saved the game. When I trotted in, the third baseman for the other team, a good friend of mine, asked, "How did you even get to that ball?"

"I don't know," I answered, "I just ran, jumped, and stretched, and bang—there was the ball."

It taught me a lesson. You never know what you can achieve if you give it that something extra.

DON'T DO ANYTHING TO CREATE BOUNDARIES.

You know we do that, don't you? We create our own limits. Our own boundaries. God—Nature—Love—Truth—have no boundaries. It is in our minds that we create these limitations and, we believe them like we believe one and one are two.

Peter Falk, the actor, has an interesting story.

It seems he traveled around a bit in his early years. He would do amateur theater in the cities where he was employed.

He had a childish and romanticized idea that ordinary people do not become actors. He placed a limit on himself.

Then one day the amateur group met with a professional group working across the street. Peter was all geared up to hear some great conversation. The first thing he heard was, "I've got to take my dirty laundry to the laundromat."

He realized professionals were ordinary people, too. The rest is history.

91

"ALL WORK AND NO PLAY" IS NOT A THOUGHT THAT LEADS TO HAPPINESS.

Neither is "all play and no work."

Somehow, we have to create a balance—a balance between work and home life.

In most cases, our workplace gets the attention while the dinner is getting cold. Continuing on that path creates bad health and even though you know you need time off, you won't ask for it because you fear for your job.

But these aren't Depression days, and employers tend to listen.

Find the harmony and balance and *hold on*.

92

TAKE A RISK. GO FOR SOMETHING YOU FEEL WILL ENRICH YOUR LIFE BUT YOU HADN'T THE COURAGE TO TRY.

Maybe there is a tremendous need to share experiences in your life, and you don't quite know how to go about it. You've thought about lecturing but you have a fear of public speaking. Find a way. Start with three people and add later.

Write a book. "Oh, I can't write," is your first reaction. That's what I thought. But here I am.

Read to children.

Teach English to those who need help.

Start a relationship with that person you've been watching for a year.

Whatever that want in your gut is . . .

Go for it now!

93

THERE IS ALWAYS THE BIGGER PICTURE, SO DON'T DESPAIR.

There is the good side to every experience in life, it's up to us to make it a habit to look for it. No matter how dire the circumstances, the bigger picture will display a good side.

For example: early in my life I went to Columbus, Ohio, to join a friend who was managing a furniture store. Although I made a good salary for a while, the store eventually closed, and I decided to leave Columbus. Things didn't look so good. I was second-guessing myself for leaving New York City.

However, it wasn't long before I found myself in Key West, Florida, broke but optimistic. It was there that one thing led to another, finally bringing me success, peace of mind, happiness, and abundance.

When things look bleak, think about the bigger picture.

JOIN IN THE MOVEMENT TO HEAL THE EARTH.

Do your part in caring for the Earth. Tune into the interconnectedness of all that exists. Uplifting the Earth in one place uplifts the Earth in all other places.

The American Indian Ojibway tribal prayer reads like this:

Grandfather.
Look at our brokenness.
We know that in all creation
Only the human family
Has strayed from the sacred way.
We know that we are the ones
Who are divided
And we are the ones
Who must come back together.
Grandfather, Sacred One
Teach us Love, Compassion, Honor

That we may heal the earth
And heal each other.

LIFE IS A SERIES OF MIRACLES.

Some positive. Some negative.

Make your life a positive miracle.

We create our own reality. That to me is a miracle, no matter what the reality may be.

You could get your Ph.D. at Harvard, or you could give up and live homeless on the streets of New York.

You could rise to the top of your profession, be it show business, or Wall Street, or medicine, or you could flounder around unable to find the key to so-called success.

Is any one of the above any more a miracle than the other? No. They are all the miracle of creation.

No matter what you have brought forth as the conditions of your life, they are the miracle of creation.

You recreate your life every day.

The miracle you seek is at your fingertips.

96

THINK POSITIVE.

We arrive on the planet with the ability to manifest our heart's desire. Whatever we desire—fame, high office, abundance—it's all there for us.

One thing stops it: negative thinking.

Let's say you have a burning desire to take an Italian vacation. And you feel really good about it. That's the key, feeling really good about it. If that's true, you will manifest your Italian trip, if there is no negative thinking going on in other areas of your life.

Even if you are feeling right about your trip, there are no misgivings, nothing negative at all. It is imperative to rid yourself of negativity concerning other areas of your life.

It may be on the job.

In your home.

Coaching Little League.

Whatever.

If negative thoughts are allowed to smolder, chances are your dream of Italy will never materialize.

Clean up the negativity in your life. It's not easy, but it can be done.

Then you will have

an Italian trip.

a South American trip.

an Australian trip.

There will be nothing to stop you.

97

KNOW THAT YOU ARE THE CAUSE OF ALL UNDESIRABLE CIRCUMSTANCES IN YOUR LIFE, AS WELL AS THE DESIRABLE.

It took a lot of years to learn that I am responsible for everything happening in my life.

I am responsible for my illnesses.

I am responsible for my predicaments.

I am responsible for my losses.

I am responsible for my gains.

I am responsible for my successes.

I am responsible for my so-called failures.

I am not a victim. That's what I would be if I placed the blame on somebody else for things that happened in my life.

Placing the blame is passing the buck and allowing others to control our life circumstances. Then, you would be the victim.

Sooner or later, we have to realize that we are doing it to ourselves. The good as well as the bad.

When we manifest unpleasantness, it's an opportunity to find a better way.

When we fail at something, it's just a learning experience. There is always the next time.

The point is this:

Look at your life and know it is your own doing.

98

EVERYTHING WE SAY, DO, THINK, AND DREAM IS A CLUE TO WHO WE ARE.

Naturally, all of the above reveal who we are. They certainly don't reveal who somebody else is.

What is our intention? It's revealed in what we say and do.

And what about our thoughts? They manifest in the physical.

So, what we see is who we are.

And now we come to dreams. Dreams are a free wheeling description of our inner lives, unencumbered by fear of censure in the waking state.

I once wrote a song entitled "Beautiful Dreams." The last lines were as follows:

 . . . Dream of a sunset in Grand Canyon
 Lonely as life with no companion
 Dream all your life and

Remember this is true
That everything in your dream
Is you.

99

WE REAP WHAT WE SOW.

Have you ever doubted that we reap what we sow?

We do! Beyond a shadow of a doubt. You plant the seed of a vegetable. You get the exact vegetable. Not another one. So be careful. You are planting seeds every moment of your existence, and those seeds will blossom. Sow bad seeds, get bad results. Sow good seeds, get good results. It makes perfect sense.

And be aware that you are planting seeds. It's important to monitor the seeds. You might ask yourself, "Why do I have to keep planting seeds?" The answer is that you can't help yourself. Every thought is a seed that will eventually blossom. So, monitor your thoughts.

As I look back over disappointing times in my life, I can plainly see that I set it all up by the seeds I planted. Of course, I didn't know it at the time. I wasn't aware that every person has her or his garden and is not going to get apples if they plant oranges.

Ask any farmer. It's his business to deal in reaping and sowing.

Thoughts are seeds. Take care when planting them.

100

ONE LAST THOUGHT: WE ARE DIVINE.

Anything that has been created contains the essence of the creator. Isn't this in evidence in our children? In our inventions? In our compositions? In our paintings? In our operas? In anything our creativity has brought about. Isn't it true that it bears the mark of our individualistic thought process. It can be no other way.

Therefore, we—being part and parcel of the universe—are divine. Being divine means sharing in the essence of our creator. The universe originated through an action of our creator. Thus, it is divine. And carrying it one step further—we are divine.

Love, being the most powerful force in the universe, shares in the divinity.

Through the practice of loving and being loved, we allow the universal love to flow through us—*and in so doing, acknowledge our awareness of being a part of the universe—a part of God. we are part of the creation of God, sharing in the divine goals of creation itself.*

That's what this book is about. To bring forth the knowing.

We are divine. We are eternal.

It is in our power to create our own lives.

Not only is it in our power to create, but we actually are creating our lives, moment to moment—unhappily in slipshod fashion, because we are unaware of our power to create. Once we truly have the crystallized awareness of this power, we can begin our quest for serenity and our march to the light. Our lives will change in overwhelming proportions. We will have entered our heaven on earth.

BIBLIOGRAPHY

Bach, Richard. *Illusions: The Adventures of a Reluctant Messiah*. Doubleday, 1977.

Chopra, Deepak. *The Seven Spiritual Laws of Success: A Practical Guide to the Fulfillment of Your Dreams*. Amber-Allen, 1995.

Dyer, Wayne. *Wisdom of the Ages: 60 Days to Enlightenment*. HarperCollins, 1998.

Foundation for Inner Peace. *A Course in Miracles*, Foundation for Inner Peace, 1975.

Gafni, Marc. *Soul Prints: Your Path to Fulfillment*. Pocket Books, 2001.

LEN CHETKIN is a retired home furnishings entrepreneur and real estate investor who owns a fine dining restaurant in western New York. His first book, *Guess Who's Jewish*, was published by the Donning Company in 1985. Married to Emmy Chetkin for thirty years, with seven children, Len Chetkin now lives in the spiritualist community of Lily Dale, New York.

Hampton Roads Publishing Company

. . . for the evolving human spirit

Hampton Roads Publishing Company
publishes books on a variety of subjects,
including metaphysics, health, integrative medicine,
visionary fiction, and other related topics.

For a copy of our latest catalog, call toll-free
800-766-8009, or send your name and address to:

Hampton Roads Publishing Company, Inc.
1125 Stoney Ridge Road
Charlottesville, VA 22902

e-mail: hrpc@hrpub.com
www.hrpub.com